I0481820

THE FIVE MINUTE FIRST TIME HOMEBUYER SPEECH

Crossing the bridge to buying your first home

John Baker

Copyright 2018
JBO Publishing Company
All Rights Reserved

For Chandler and Camryn
Who inspire me every day

The information contained within this book is strictly for educational purposes. If you wish to apply ideas contained herin, you are taking full responsibility for your actions.

The author has made every effort to ensure the accuracy of the information within this book was correct at time of publication. The author does not assume and hereby disclaims any liability to any party for any loss, damage, or disruption caused by errors or omissions, whether such errors or omissions result from accident, negligence, or any other cause.

No part of this book may be reproduced or transmitted in any form or by any means, electronic or mechanical, including photocopying, recording or by any information storage and retrieval system, without written permission from the author.

THE FIVE MINUTE FIRST TIME HOMEBUYER SPEECH

Crossing the bridge to buying your first home

John Baker

Introduction

I have been involved in the banking, financial services and mortgage industry for over twenty years. Almost every day, I talk to a potential first time homebuyer. I used to ask them, "What questions do you have about the home buying process?" Most would answer something along the lines of, "I don't even know what to ask!" After hundreds of those conversations, explaining the basic process over and over again, I had developed what I began to refer to as, my "first time homebuyer's speech." This short explanation will walk you through the basic steps it takes to see if you are ready to begin the process of getting pre-qualified, and it will probably answer most of the basic questions you may already have. Once we have gone through this process, you will know if you are ready, and even if it's not quite the right time, I will give you some information, goals and tools so that you can be ready in the future.

None of what I talk about is a secret, mortgage loans have basically worked the same for a long time. I will break down the process, so that it is easy to understand precisely the steps that need to be taken to get pre-approved, or as I like to refer to those steps, the bridges that need to be crossed.

Most people begin to think about buying a home, when their income situation seems steady and they are looking at settling down. They have a steady stream of income they feel confident about continuing, they may be saving some money, or maybe they are needing more space for a growing family. They begin to discuss buying instead of renting, and may even start looking at houses online. They eventually reach out to a real estate agent, who pretty early on in the conversation asks, "Have you been pre-qualified by a lender yet?" That's where I come in.

The first step to buying a home is to get pre-qualified, or pre-approved, by a lender. This is simply where we take an application, ask you some questions, check your credit, and hopefully give you a letter that says that the bank will loan you up to a certain amount to purchase your house. You then give a copy of this letter to your real estate agent, and off you go to find your dream home. So what really matters at this point is, how do you get that letter? Well, to get that letter, we have to cross four bridges. I mentioned the first one already, your credit score.

Did you know that 74% of renters wish to buy a home, but are afraid they won't qualify, so they never even try.
(National Association of Realtors Homebuyer Statistics)

Bridge 1
Credit Score

We all know the importance of having a good credit score, but let's face it, life happens. I think this is probably the most intimidating part of taking that first step to becoming a homeowner. In fact, it stops many people from ever making that first call to a real estate agent or lender. Many people think that you need to have perfect credit in order to buy a house, and they never even take a shot at buying, because they know they have had some credit issues in the past. I have gotten many buyers into a home that admit they really didn't think they would ever be able to qualify.

There are many programs and options for people that have less than perfect credit scores. I am not going to go into all of those in this book, but let's just say that you want your credit score to be somewhere above 580. You will have even more options if you have a score that is at least 620.

There may be some options if you have a lower score, but in general, this is a good place to start. Your score will affect your rate and other loan terms, so the higher your score, the better your options are going to be.

We are going to pull your score from all three credit bureaus, Equifax, Experian and Transunion. We throw out the highest score, and we throw out the lowest score, and we use the score that is in the middle. If there is more than one borrower, we will use the lower of those middle scores for the loan. There are many ways today to check your credit score, a FICO score from a credit card for example, but we won't actually know what that middle score is until a mortgage lender pulls your credit, and then we go from there.

Let's look at this credit score in a little more detail. I must mention at this point, that I am not a credit advisor, the tips I give in this section just come from my years of experience in lending and my own observations. If your score is not quite there yet, don't give up. There are many things you can do to try and bring your score up. Many people have had some issues in the past, and simply don't use credit anymore. It's hard to re-establish a good pay history, if you don't use credit at all.

Most banks and credit unions these days offer a "secured credit card." You put an amount, something like $300, in your checking or savings account, the bank puts a hold on that amount, and they issue you a $300 credit card. The key here is going to be to keep a very low balance, like 10%. So, keep about $30 on the card, pay the minimum payments each month, and when it is almost paid off, go put another $30 on the card. This can help show the giant credit computer in the sky, that you know how to manage credit and make your payments on time as agreed, and as the months go by, this can help your credit scores rise. Be careful though, if you max it out, it will have the opposite effect, so the key is keeping a low balance.

Maybe you already have some credit card debt. Make sure those payments are being made on time, and again, try to get the balances as low as possible. The more available credit you have on those cards, the further the balances are from the limit, the better that looks for your credit score. Also, consider paying off any charged off accounts, especially any of the smaller ones. Medical bills may affect your credit score, but most lenders aren't going to require you to pay off medical debts. There are programs available even if you have had foreclosures or a bankruptcy in the past. Generally, as long as they are now settled and in the past, there may be a program that will work with you.

Judgements, such as tax liens, will need to be cleared up first.

Hopefully, you are reading this and thinking, "Okay, no problem so far, I have perfect credit!" That's great, let's move on to bridge number two. You need to have some type of income, and it needs to be enough to pay your bills.

Did you know, 54% of first time home buyers are married?

(National Association of Realtors Homebuyer Statistics)

Bridge 2
Income

I think that this is often the easiest bridge to cross for most people. I simply mean most people who are thinking about buying a home, have a steady stream of income, and are wanting to use this income wisely by purchasing a home. Hopefully, they are even establishing some savings as well. There are several different ways people earn income, and this matters when it comes to figuring out how much your gross monthly income is, and therefore, how much house you can afford.

The most common income types are W2 incomes, like salary and hourly wage employees, self-employed individuals, and those who receive a passive income, like Social Security, retirements, etc.

For those who get paid a yearly salary, simply divide that by twelve to find your gross monthly income. If you get paid hourly and work a normal forty hour week, multiply your hourly rate times forty, then multiply that times 52, then divide that by twelve.

If you are a W2 employee, you will likely need to show your last year's W2, and your last thirty days of pay stubs to show your income. Your lender will want to know your job history for the last 24 months.

It's worth noting here that if you just graduated and recently started working, you should be okay.
For instance, you just graduated college a few months ago to become a teacher, and now you are teaching, that should work just fine.
Perhaps you have a part time job.
Your lender will probably be able to use that as long as you have had that job for at least two years. If you have been there less than two years, you probably can't use that income.

If you happen to be self-employed, things work a little differently. The lender will want to see the last two years of tax returns for you and maybe even your business, depending on how your business is set up.
This often presents a problem, because as a business owner, you often try to claim as little

income as possible on your tax returns. Your income will be determined by what you have claimed as your personal income on your last two tax returns.

This means you need to have been in this position long enough to have filed at least two tax returns, and also that those returns have to show enough income to qualify you.

Your accountant can give you advice on how you can make sure you are claiming enough income to be in a position to obtain financing, for a home or otherwise.

There are other kinds of income that are okay to use as well, such as Social Security, retirements, etc. You will be required to show your awards letter from the source of this income, and that letter will need to show that there is a likelihood that the income will continue. In other words, it can't be temporary.

Figuring out your gross monthly income is how the lender determines exactly how much house you can buy.

We figure that out with this fancy banking term we call, "debt to income ratio," or DTI. This simply means that your monthly income has to be enough for you to pay this new mortgage, and whatever other payments you have, like cars and credit cards. Again, there are different programs that offer many different options here, but let's just say you want that number to be about 45% or less of your monthly gross income.

So let's do some math! Add up your monthly payments for things like car payments, student loans, credit cards, etc. Not your cable bill or electric bill or things like that. Also add in what you think your mortgage payment will be. (There are many calculators online that can give you an idea of what your payment will look like, don't forget about the taxes and insurance.) Now take that number, and divide it by your gross monthly income, before anything is taken out, that is your debt to income ratio. Just like with the credit score, we can talk about what it might be all day long, but completing an application and looking at your credit report and income information will get us an accurate number for what you qualify for.

It may be that you want buy something in the $300k range, and you end up qualifying for something a little less, or a little more, but completing the application will give you the answers as to exactly how much house you can afford at this time.

So far, so good, right? Rolling right along, we have two bridges left to cross, and they are kind of related. They can also be the most difficult to get across. But as always, we have lots of options, so let's go to bridge number three. You need to have some money saved up to use for a down payment.

Did you know, 35% of all home buyers, are buying their first home?

(National Association of Realtors Homebuyer Statistics)

Bridge 3
Down payment

Again, there are a lot of different options here, with many different programs offered by different lenders which I am not going to go into specifically. I am going to go through the general requirements when it comes to the down payment on a typical loan.

Let me begin this section by saying there are many different federal, state, county and city down payment assistance programs that may be available to assist with your down payment, they each have their own minimums and requirements to qualify. There are also common loan programs, like VA and USDA loans that will allow you to borrow 100% with no down payment, but you must meet certain conditions, like being active military or a veteran, or buying a home in a rural area and meeting certain income requirements.

Assuming we are not going any of those routes, I am going to discuss what you need to have in general for down payment money.
You typically will need to have at least 3.5% of

the purchase price for a down payment. The lender will want to see two months of bank statements to show that you have at least this amount of funds, and that you have had this money for at least the last two months.

If there are any large deposits shown in those statements, you will be required to show where the money in those deposits came from. In most cases, this down payment money can be a gift, say from Mom and Dad, and they will need to sign a letter that says the money is a gift and that you will not be required to repay this gift. The person giving the gift will also need to show where that money is coming from, as in two months of their own bank statements.

You will likely be required to pay PMI, private mortgage insurance, if you borrow anything over 80%, meaning that you put down less than 20%. PMI is basically insurance for the lender that helps cover them if your loan goes into default, and it is added to your monthly mortgage payment along with your taxes and insurance.

Your rate is also affected by down payment. A good way to look at it is to simply say, the more money you put down, the better, but 3.5% will get you started. Most first time home buyers aren't going to have 20%, which is why these programs exist.

So now we are down to the fourth and final bridge to cross, and as I mentioned earlier, it is related to the third bridge. You have to have money to use for closing costs.

Did you know, 24% of first time home buyers used gift funds from a parent or family member?

(National Association of Realtors Homebuyer Statistics)

Bridge 4
Closing Costs

We talked about the money you need to have in the bank for your down payment, and you also need to have enough funds in your accounts to cover your closing costs. There are many different people and services that are required to complete a mortgage loan transaction, and all of those people want to get paid for their services. You will be charged for things like your credit report, your appraisal, property inspections, the title company/attorney that will handle the title work and the closing on your loan, and a loan origination fee paid to the lender, just to name a few. These costs are generally going to start around $2500-$3000, depending on your loan size.

As a first time home buyer, you will be required to pay your property taxes and homeowner's insurance as a part of your monthly payment, a fancy banking term we call "escrow." The lender will take your annual property taxes and homeowner's insurance premium, and divide that into a monthly escrow payment, which will be added to your principal and interest payment. They will want to include a couple of months of reserves, to ensure that there will be enough money in that escrow account to be able to pay those amounts when they are due. All of this, when added to your down payment requirement, can be several thousand dollars. For math's sake, let's use $100k for a purchase price. You will need about $3500 for closing costs, and for your escrow pre-paids. Don't forget that you will need $3500 for your down payment, a total of around $7000.

Here is where I hope I can make it a little better than it may sound. Probably about 80% of the purchase contracts that come across my desk, have the seller paying a portion of those closing costs. For example, you find the perfect house, you make an offer, and you ask in your offer that the seller pay a portion of your closing costs. Generally, depending on your loan program and how much you are putting down, this can be from 3%-6%. You will be required to pay your down payment portion, either from your funds or gift funds, then the seller can pay part of the other costs. Let's go back to our $100k scenario. You would need to come up with the $3500 for the down payment, you could ask the seller to pay 3%, or $3000, which almost gets you to the approximate $7000 you need. In this case, if they will pay $3000, you can pay about $4000, and you are all set! The downside to this is that until you find a specific property with that particular seller, you won't know if that is going to be possible. The seller may not be in a position to be able pay anything at all, or may be limited as to how much they can contribute, but this is why it is so important to have a knowledgeable real estate agent to assist you with the negotiations when you are going through the home buying process.

Summary

That is it, we have crossed all four bridges! At this point, I hope you have a better idea of whether or not you are ready to take the first steps and apply for a pre-approval letter. If you think you have some areas to work on, at least I hope to have helped you come up with a game plan to get you ready to buy in the near future. I have had many clients that called me back a few weeks or months after we first spoke, and said that they were finally ready to get that application going, and they are homeowners now.

Again, the things I have gone through in this book are a general snapshot of what to expect, there are many different kinds of programs and options that may be able to help you.

It is so very important to work with a knowledgeable and trustworthy loan officer to help you through the pre-approval process, all the way until your loan closes. It is just as important to find a real estate agent that offers the same.

Find someone who listens to what you want to

do, what you are looking for, someone who can answer all of your questions, and can present you with options and scenarios that make sure you get into the house and the loan that is best for you.

I hope I have helped break down this process, and good luck on crossing the bridge to buying your first home.

THE FIVE MINUTE FIRST TIME HOMEBUYER SPEECH

Crossing the bridge to buying your first home

John Baker

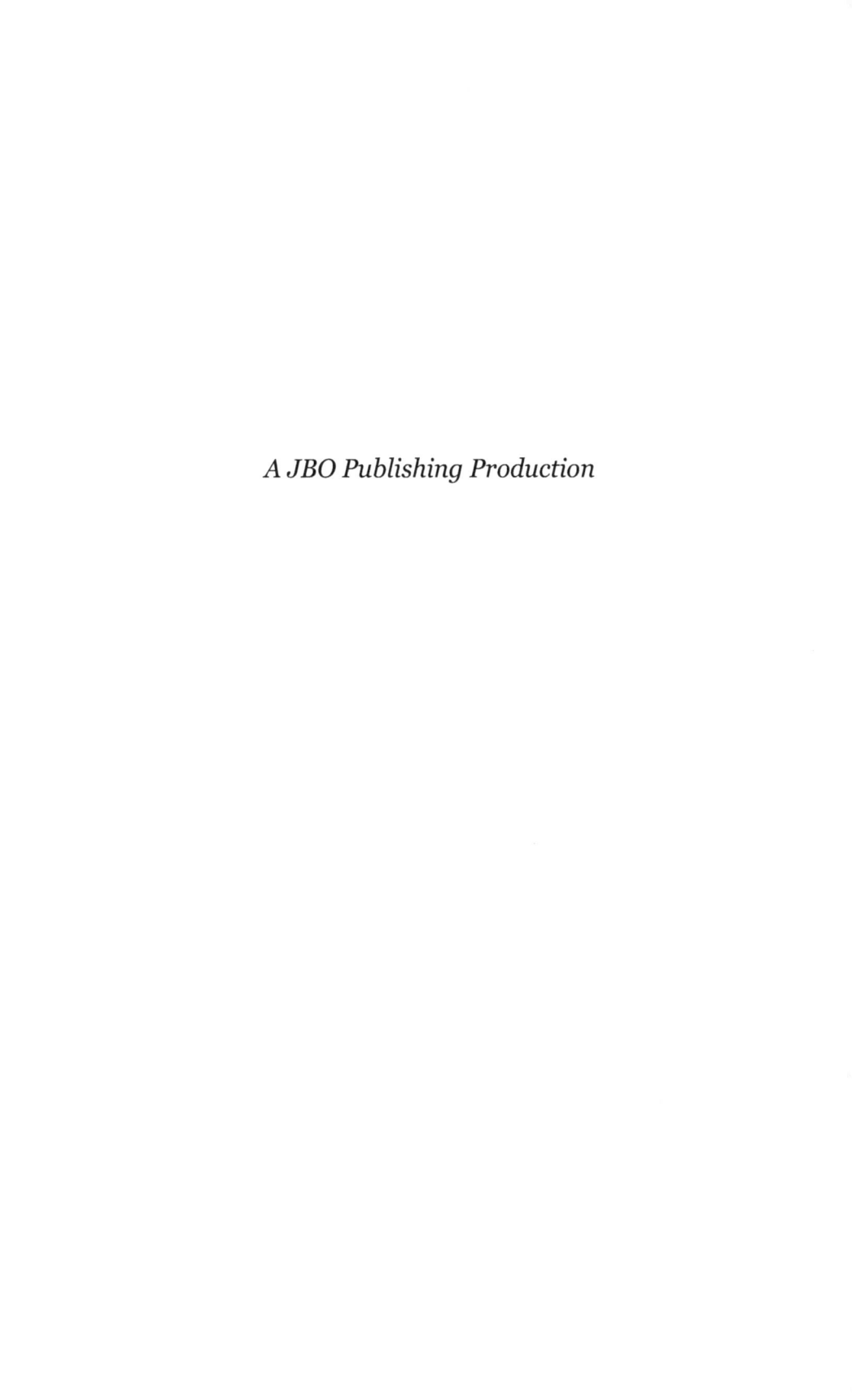

A JBO Publishing Production

www.ingramcontent.com/pod-product-compliance
Lightning Source LLC
Chambersburg PA
CBHW072048230526
45468CB00019B/1049